Progress In Learning

Book 1

An easy-to-use workbook to improve reading,
writing and listening

by

KIM MORRIS

Specialist in working with children who have dyslexia and
associated learning difficulties

For more information on educational resources, visit:

www.progressinlearning.co.nz

This book belongs to:

_____

Tel no: _____

<u>Dedication</u>

This book is dedicated to my student, Troy Wigley, who has shown immense courage and tenacity in his efforts to overcome a severe learning disability. A true hero!

Contents

Introduction

This programme is based on a common-sense approach to reading using a structure and cumulative phonic system of word patterns. Irregular words that occur in the English language are gradually introduced and the students are taught to decode longer multisyllabic words as the reading series progresses.

The book is an invaluable resource for use within the context of the regular classroom and in working with those children and adults who are dyslexic.

Purpose of the Book

This book can be used to teach students how to:

- Read faster

- Read with greater accuracy

- Decode longer words

- Spell with greater accuracy

- Write simple sentences correctly

- Listen more effectively

- Understand the meaning of simple sentences

About the Author

Credentials

- H.D.E. Junior Primary
- F.D.E. Remedial Education
- B.A. Degree
- SPELD NZ Certificate Course in Specific Learning Disabilities
- Color of Woman, Intentional Creativity Teacher

Kim Morris is a specialist teacher, trained to work with children who have dyslexia and associated learning difficulties.

Kim completed a four-year diploma in Junior Primary education at the Johannesburg College of Education in 1982. Early on in her teaching career she was drawn to working with children who presented with specific learning disabilities or dyslexia, so she specialised in remedial education, completing a diploma in Remedial Education and a BA degree.

Kim has many years of teaching experience, mostly in working with children who have perceptual and learning difficulties. This enables her to play a vital role in identifying and meeting their learning needs in the regular classroom.

Her experience includes working as a remedial teacher under the supervision of the Newlands Child Guidance Clinic in Cape Town and teaching at Crossroads Remedial School in Johannesburg. Kim spent 7 years in Zimbabwe where she founded and ran the Remedial Centre at St. John's Preparatory School in Harare.

On her return to South Africa, she worked as the remedial teacher at Noordhoek Private School.

Immigrating to New Zealand in 2003, Kim returned to mainstream teaching where she was employed as a class teacher in South Auckland for four years, teaching at Manurewa West Primary and at St. John the Evangelist School. This enabled her to become familiar with the New Zealand curriculum and obtain full teacher registration.

Kim completed a SPELD NZ Certificate Course in Specific Learning Disabilities in 2007 and has since been actively involved in the learning community, tutoring students, presenting in service training to teachers on topics relating to dyslexia, and supporting the students in the regular classroom and at home.

Kim is a certified Intentional Creativity Teacher and has published the Wings to Fly, fun coloring and activity journal for children, which promotes health and wellbeing.

As founder of Progress In Learning, Kim provides educational resources designed to be affordable and accessible to all communities. This empowers others to make a difference in their lives.

Who Would Benefit from Using the Book?

The book is suitable for:

- Parents to use with their children who have reading, writing or language difficulties.

- Dyslexic students who are reading below the expected level of achievement.

- Teachers, teacher aides and specialist teachers who work with dyslexic children as part of their reading and writing programme at home and at school.

- Students who are reading adequately but wish to accelerate their progress.

- Teachers who need a list of words which are taught systematically and in word families.

- Peer tutors who may wish to help younger or less able students read more effectively.

- Adult literacy students.

Where to Start

Visit www.progressinlearning.co.nz to view and download the free PIL Phonic Skills Check, which can be used to determine placement within the programme.

The assessment provides valuable information as to where and why a student is struggling and indicates which sounds need revision.

The PIL Phonic Skills Check includes instruction sheets, student sheets and tester sheets. Progress can be monitored by termly reassessment or when a book has been completed.

How to Record the Reading Progress

View an example of the completed grid on page 14.

The objective is for the student to read the list words and sentences correctly on three consecutive days.

The First Day

- The tutor is seated to the top right of the student.
- Record the date at the top of the list.
- Ask the student to read the list of letter sounds or words downwards.
- Score a vertical line as shown (|) if the student reads the word correctly.
- If a word is not read correctly, ask the student to try again. Draw a dot (·) if the word is not read correctly the second time. Tell the student what the word was.
- The student needs to practice reading the words or sounds in which errors were made by writing them out a few times on a piece of paper and saying the word or sound as it is written.
- When the student has completed one list, move onto the next list and complete it in the same way.
- Each list should only be attempted once per day.
- Ask the student to read the sentences below the word list.

- Record any errors such as insertions, substitutions or omissions made above the sentence and provide immediate feedback and training to correct this.
- Do approximately 3 pages of the book daily.

The Second and Third Day

- Go to the starting point for the first day.
- Record the date at the top of the list, next to the previous date.
- Repeat the process as for the first day.

After That

- If necessary, repeat as for the first three days, leaving out the reading of the words which have been read correctly on three consecutive days.
- Students whose reading lacks fluency may need to spend time reading the lists and sentences under timed conditions.

Note

The amount of work covered and the number of repetitions of word lists required may be adapted to suit the needs of the child.

Example of a Completed Grid

List 13	3/5	4/5	5/5	6/5	List 14	3/5	4/5	5/5		List 15	3/5	4/5	5/5	
-at	I	I	I		-ap	I	I	I		-an	I	I	I	
bat	I	I	I		yap	I	I	I		ban	I	I	I	
cat	·	I	I	I	cap	I	I	I		fan	I	I	I	
fat	I	I	I		gap	I	I	I		can	I	I	I	
hat	·	I	I	I	lap	I	I	I		man	I	I	I	
mat	I	I	I		map	I	I	I		nan	I	I	I	
pat	I	I	I		nap	I	I	I		pan	I	I	I	
rat	I	I	I		rap	I	I	I		ran	I	I	I	
sat	I	I	I		sap	I	I	I		tan	I	I	I	
vat	I	I	I		tap	I	I	I		van	I	I	I	
lat	I	I	I		zap	·	I	I	I	yan	·	I	I	I

The fat cat had a nap on my lap.

Pat had a very big map in the tan van.

My Progress Chart

Date started: ....

Unit 1	-	The Alphabet and Chart	☐
Unit 2	-	Two-Letter Words and Pseudo Words	☐
Unit 3	-	Rime Chunks Chart A	☐
Unit 4	-	Three-Letter Words	☐
Unit 5	-	High-Frequency Words 1-20	☐
Unit 6	-	Plural-s	☐
Unit 7	-	High-Frequency Words 21-40	☐
Unit 8	-	Rime Chunks Chart B	☐
Unit 9	-	Initial Consonant Blends	☐
Unit 10	-	High-Frequency Words 41-60	☐
Unit 11	-	Final Double Consonants	☐
Unit 12	-	High-Frequency Words 61-80	☐
Unit 13	-	Final Consonant Blends	☐
Unit 14	-	High-Frequency Words 81-100	☐

Date finished: ....

Unit 1: The Alphabet Picture Chart 1

a A	b B	c C	d D
e E	f F	g G	h H
i I	j J	k K	l L
m M			

The Alphabet Picture Chart 2

n N	o O	p P	q Q
r R	s S	t T	u U
v V	w W	x X	y Y
		box	
z Z			

Unit 1: The Alphabet

List 1					List 2					List 3				
a					q					G				
b					r					H				
c					s					I				
d					t					J				
e					u					K				
f					v					L				
g					w					M				
h					x					N				
i					y					O				
j					z					P				
k					A					Q				
l					B					R				
m					C					S				
n					D					T				
o					E					U				
p					F					V				

The Alphabet

List 4				List 5					List 6				
W				b					b or d ?				
X				z					b				
y				e					d				
Z				v					b				
Mixed alphabet				h					d				
k				s					d				
d				u					b				
x				p					b				
g				t					d				
m				c					b				
j				f					d				
y				i					b				
o				l					d				
a				n					d				
r				q					d				
w				m					b				

Unit 2: Two-Letter Words and Pseudo Words

List 7					List 8					List 9				
a-					e-					o-				
am					el					on				
an					es					off				
as					ef					ox				
at					et					ol				
al					ep					od				
ap					ev					om				
ag					eg					ob				
ad					ex					ock				
af					ed					op				
aj					en					os				
ab					eb					ot				
ack					eck					ov				
av					em					oz				
ax					ej					og				
az					ez					os				

Two-Letter Words and Pseudo Words

List 10				List 11				List 12			
i-				u-				Mixed Word List			
it				us				ag			
is				up				ef			
if				uf				ix			
in				ut				ol			
il				ul				ud			
ip				uv				af			
ig				ug				eb			
id				ux				ick			
im				ud				op			
ix				un				un			
ib				ub				al			
ick				uck				ev			
iv				um				im			
ij				uf				og			
iz				uz				ub			

Unit 3: Rime Chunks Chart A

Learn to read these downwards, across and in step fashion.

an	at	ad	ag	ab	am	ap
en	et	ed	eg	eb	em	ep
on	ot	od	og	ob	om	op
in	it	id	ig	ib	im	ip
un	ut	ud	ug	ub	um	up

Unit 4: Short Vowel -a- as in apple

List 13				List 14				List 15			
-at				-ap				-an			
bat				yap				ban			
cat				cap				fan			
fat				gap				can			
hat				lap				man			
mat				map				nan			
pat				nap				pan			
rat				rap				ran			
sat				sap				tan			
vat				tap				van			
fat				zap				dan			

The fat cat had a nap in my lap.

Pat had a big map in the tan van.

Short Vowel -a- as in apple

List 16					List 17					List 18				
-af					-ab					-al				
baf					tab					pal				
caf					fab					gal				
daf					cab					cal				
faf					nab					mal				
gaf					dab					nal				
laf					jab					ral				
maf					lab					val				
raf					gab					tal				
saf					hab					yal				
taf					sab					fal				

The rat and the fat cat got a tab.

Pat and his pal got the sad cat.

Short Vowel -a- as in apple

List 19					List 20					List 21				
-ad					-ag					-am				
bad					bag					dam				
cad					gag					ham				
fad					hag					jam				
had					lag					ram				
lad					mag					cam				
mad					nag					yam				
pad					rag					fam				
sad					sag					pam				
dad					tag					wam				
rad					wag					mam				

Sam and Pam had a bag of yams.

Dad had the wet rag in the van.

Short Vowel -a- as in apple

List 22				List 23				List 24				
-as				-av				-ax				
gas				cav				fax				
pas				fav				wax				
cas				jav				lax				
fas				lav				tax				
las				tav				pax				
mas				mav				dax				
ras				sav				hax				
sas				wav				cax				
tas				bav				gax				
nas				yav				jax				

Nan can get to the gas man.

Dan has the jam in the tan van.

Short Vowel -a- as in apple

List 25					List 26					List 27				
-az					Mixed Word List					Mixed Word List				
gaz					cat					has				
faz					ham					pat				
daz					jab					lab				
raz					lag					jam				
taz					tan					sap				
caz					mat					pal				
laz					sag					hag				
paz					wax					pan				
jaz					pad					fax				
maz					yap					jab				

Pam ran to get the ham in the pan.

Al and his pal can pat the wet dog.

Short Vowel -e- as in elephant

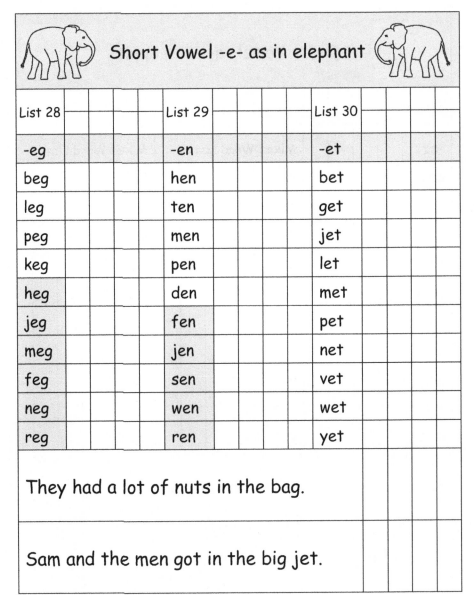

List 28				List 29				List 30			
-eg				-en				-et			
beg				hen				bet			
leg				ten				get			
peg				men				jet			
keg				pen				let			
heg				den				met			
jeg				fen				pet			
meg				jen				net			
feg				sen				vet			
neg				wen				wet			
reg				ren				yet			

They had a lot of nuts in the bag.

Sam and the men got in the big jet.

Short Vowel -e- as in elephant

List 31				List 32				List 33			
-eb				-ef				-em			
web				ref				hem			
feb				fef				lem			
heb				hef				jem			
leb				lef				sem			
meb				mef				tem			
peb				nef				fem			
neb				tef				nem			
beb				pef				pem			
jeb				sef				rem			
zeb				vef				wem			

Deb and Jim ran to the web.

Can I get the hem up?

Short Vowel -e- as in elephant

List 34				List 35				List 36				
-el				-ep				-es				
bel				pep				yes				
sel				rep				wes				
vel				jep				tes				
jel				lep				ves				
mel				mep				fes				
nel				fep				jes				
pel				nep				les				
fel				hep				mes				
hel				sep				res				
rel				tep				nes				

The fat cat got the bug on the web.

Dan had a pet dog and a pet cat.

Short Vowel -e- as in elephant

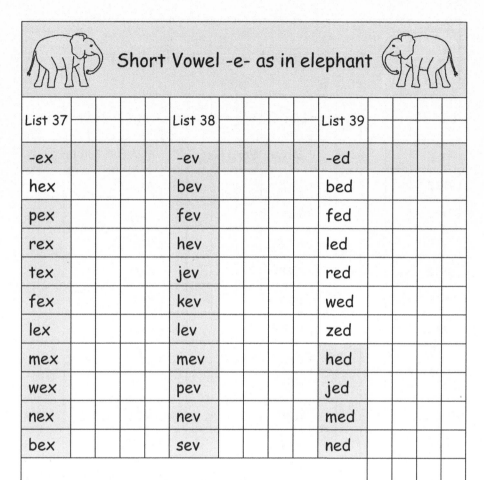

List 37				List 38				List 39			
-ex				-ev				-ed			
hex				bev				bed			
pex				fev				fed			
rex				hev				led			
tex				jev				red			
fex				kev				wed			
lex				lev				zed			
mex				mev				hed			
wex				pev				jed			
nex				nev				med			
bex				sev				ned			

Rex fed the pet on the wet mat.

Bev can get the red net and the pen.

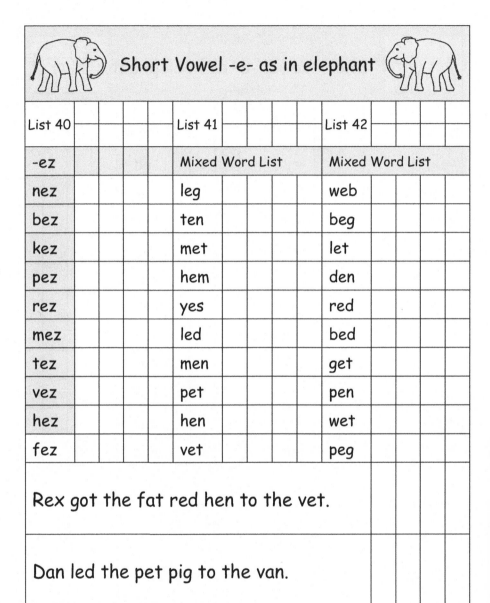

Short Vowel -e- as in elephant

List 40					List 41					List 42				
-ez					Mixed Word List					Mixed Word List				
nez					leg					web				
bez					ten					beg				
kez					met					let				
pez					hem					den				
rez					yes					red				
mez					led					bed				
tez					men					get				
vez					pet					pen				
hez					hen					wet				
fez					vet					peg				

Rex got the fat red hen to the vet.

Dan led the pet pig to the van.

Short Vowel -o- as in octopus

List 43				List 44				List 45			
-ob				-ox				-of			
cob				box				cof			
fob				fox				dof			
job				pox				pof			
lob				lox				lof			
mob				mox				sof			
rob				tox				gof			
sob				vox				hof			
bob				rox				mof			
hob				jox				rof			
tob				yox				fof			

The fox and the cub ran in the den.

Bob and Pam got the lid on the box.

Short Vowel -o- as in octopus

List 46				List 47				List 48				
-og				-ol				-om				
cog				fol				com				
dog				sol				dom				
fog				hol				fom				
log				jol				hom				
hog				col				lom				
jog				dol				pom				
bog				lol				rom				
sog				mol				som				
yog				pol				tom				
nog				rol				wom				

The dog ran to the log in the fog.

The lid is on top of the box.

Short Vowel -o- as in octopus

List 49				List 50				List 51			
-od				-on				-op			
cod				con				cop			
nod				don				hop			
pod				non				lop			
rod				hon				mop			
sod				bon				pop			
god				mon				top			
bod				lon				sop			
lod				gon				fop			
fod				pon				nop			
dod				fon				rop			

Don got the rod and the net.

Pam can hop up to the top.

Short Vowel -o- as in octopus

List 52				List 53				List 54			
-os				-ot				-oz			
cos				cot				foz			
hos				dot				goz			
tos				got				hoz			
bos				hot				joz			
jos				jot				loz			
fos				lot				moz			
mos				not				noz			
gos				pot				poz			
nos				rot				roz			
yos				tot				toz			

The fox ran in the box and had the cod.

Dot said that he is on the big TV.

Mixed Word Lists

List 55					List 56					List 57				
Mixed Word List					Mixed Word List					Mixed Word List				
rob					rat					bag				
fox					leg					ten				
hog					got					not				
rod					fan					tan				
mop					red					hem				
lot					hop					fog				
sob					can					fax				
box					bed					hen				
log					rot					dog				
top					ram					fat				

The ham can rot in the hot sun.

The red pen is in my bag.

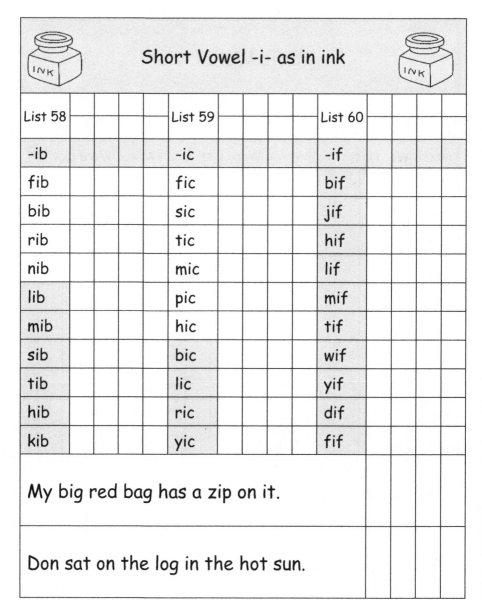

Short Vowel -i- as in ink

List 58				List 59				List 60				
-ib				-ic				-if				
fib				fic				bif				
bib				sic				jif				
rib				tic				hif				
nib				mic				lif				
lib				pic				mif				
mib				hic				tif				
sib				bic				wif				
tib				lic				yif				
hib				ric				dif				
kib				yic				fif				

My big red bag has a zip on it.

Don sat on the log in the hot sun.

Short Vowel -i- as in ink

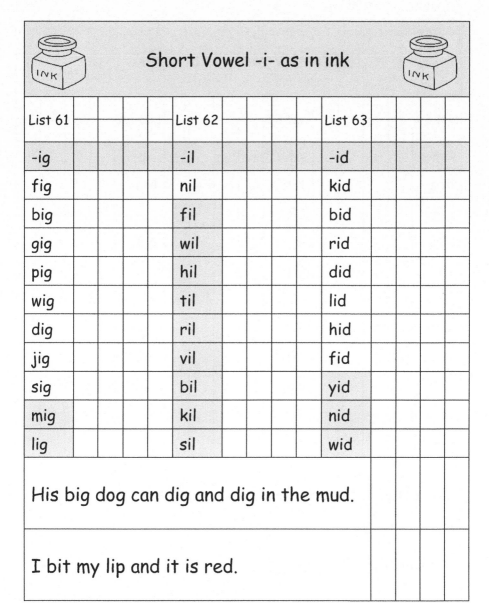

List 61				List 62				List 63			
-ig				-il				-id			
fig				nil				kid			
big				fil				bid			
gig				wil				rid			
pig				hil				did			
wig				til				lid			
dig				ril				hid			
jig				vil				fid			
sig				bil				yid			
mig				kil				nid			
lig				sil				wid			

His big dog can dig and dig in the mud.

I bit my lip and it is red.

Short Vowel -i- as in ink

List 64				List 65				List 66				
-im				-it				-ip				
him				fit				hip				
dim				bit				lip				
rim				lit				pip				
sim				pit				rip				
jim				sit				sip				
kim				wit				tip				
lim				hit				nip				
fim				vit				dip				
mim				mit				zip				
pim				jit				vip				

They had a dip in the dam as it was hot.

A big dog was at the tip.

Short Vowel -i- as in ink

List 67					List 68					List 69				
-in					-is					-iv				
fin					his					miv				
bin					wis					div				
win					mis					niv				
tin					dis					fiv				
pin					nis					riv				
sin					tis					giv				
din					vis					hiv				
min					fis					siv				
kin					lis					tiv				
hin					ris					yiv				

She hid the wig in the bed.

His kit bag is in the cab.

Short Vowel -i- as in ink

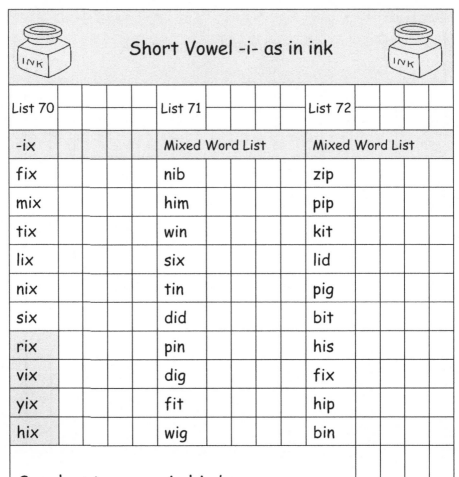

List 70				List 71				List 72			
-ix				Mixed Word List				Mixed Word List			
fix				nib				zip			
mix				him				pip			
tix				win				kit			
lix				six				lid			
nix				tin				pig			
six				did				bit			
rix				pin				his			
vix				dig				fix			
yix				fit				hip			
hix				wig				bin			

Sam has ten pens in his bag.

The big red hat did not fit him.

Short Vowel -u- as in umbrella

List 73				List 74				List 75			
-ut				-ug				-up			
cut				hug				cup			
gut				bug				pup			
hut				lug				yup			
nut				mug				gup			
rut				dug				sup			
but				tug				tup			
jut				jug				lup			
tut				rug				bup			
sut				vug				fup			
yut				yug				rup			

They can hop and run in the sun.

The pup got wet in the dam.

Short Vowel -u- as in umbrella

List 76					List 77					List 78				
-ud					-uf					-ul				
cud					cuf					gul				
dud					puf					hul				
mud					duf					dul				
bud					suf					cul				
fud					ruf					tul				
gud					luf					nul				
hud					muf					mul				
jud					tuf					rul				
lud					yuf					sul				
pud					guf					ful				

The dog and the fox ran in the mud.

It is not wet in the hut.

Short Vowel -u- as in umbrella

List 79				List 80				List 81				
-um				-ub				-us				
gum				rub				bus				
hum				tub				pus				
mum				cub				fus				
sum				dub				gus				
yum				hub				lus				
tum				pub				mus				
rum				sub				rus				
fum				vub				hus				
num				yub				jus				
lum				lub				cus				

I can go in the bus but not the van.

Ned has a cat on his lap.

Short Vowel -u- as in umbrella

List 82				List 83				List 84				
-un				-uv				-uc				
fun				luv				huc				
run				guv				duc				
bun				muv				muc				
nun				suv				ruc				
gun				ruv				luc				
pun				tuv				juc				
sun				fuv				nuc				
tun				duv				puc				
vun				yuv				suc				
hun				huv				tuc				

Jan and Sam had fun in the sun.

The man hid the gun in the hut.

Short Vowel -u- as in umbrella

List 85				List 86				List 87				
-ux				-uz				Mixed Word List				
lux				luz				map				
tux				nuz				jet				
mux				tuz				him				
yux				muz				pen				
pux				buz				man				
hux				fuz				not				
bux				suz				rug				
jux				ruz				sit				
nux				puz				rod				
rux				cuz				hum				

A big jet can go up and up.

Jen had a red cap on.

Unit 5: High-Frequency Words 1-20

List 88					List 89					
the					was					
and					you					
a					they					
to					on					
said					she					
in					is					
he					for					
I					at					
of					his					
it					but					
She can get to the dog.										
That was my pen in the bag.										

Unit 6: Plurals -s

List 90				List 91				List 92			
-s				-s				-s			
dog				pen				bin			
dogs				pens				bins			
net				bun				leg			
nets				buns				legs			
pig				fig				pot			
pigs				figs				pots			
mat				log				fan			
mats				logs				fans			
nut				hat				hug			
nuts				hats				hugs			

Pets can be a lot of fun.

I have ten rats and six hens.

Unit 7: High-Frequency Words 21-40

List 93					List 94				
that					what				
with					there				
all					out				
we					this				
can					have				
are					went				
up					be				
had					like				
my					some				
her					so				

We went over there to have some fun.

Ben sat on the log and had some nuts.

Unit 8: Rime Chunks Chart B
Learn to read these downwards, across and in step fashion.

ack	amp	all	ing	ank	eet	and
eck	emp	ell	ang	ink	eem	end
ock	omp	oll	ong	unk	eep	oss
ick	imp	ill	ung	ent	eek	ess
uck	ump	ull	est	ust	eed	uff

Unit 9: Initial Blends Picture Chart 1

fl	gl	bl
flag	glove	block
cl	pl	sl
clock	planet	slide
br	cr	dr
brush	crab	dragon
fr	pr	gr
frog	present	grapes

Initial Blends Picture Chart 2

tr	wh	sw
tree	wheel	swim
tw	dw	sc
twin	dwarf	scarecrow
sn	sk	sp
snow	skull	spot
st	sm	
stop	smile	

Initial Blend fl- as in flag

List 95					List 96				
fl-					fl-				
flag					flip				
flap					flips				
flan					flick				
flat					flint				
fled					fling				
flex					flum				
flop					flig				
floss					flot				
flock					flep				
flog					flup				

The red flag can flap in the wind.

A frog can jump and hop to the pond.

Initial Blend gl- as in glove

List 97					List 98				
gl-					Mixed Word List				
glad					flag				
gland					glum				
glass					flop				
glint					glut				
gloss					flex				
glut					glass				
glum					fling				
glop					gland				
glam					flip				
glands					glad				
We will be glum if we do not win.									
I am glad Tom got the pup.									

Initial Blend bl- as in block

List 99					List 100				
bl-					bl-				
block					bless				
blocks					blend				
blob					black				
blot					blab				
blots					blank				
bluff					blip				
bliss					blaf				
blink					blet				
blinks					blom				
bled					blug				

The long cut bled a lot.

The black duck did not blink at all.

Initial Blend cl- as in clock								
List 101				List 102				
cl-				cl-				
clock				clip				
clog				cling				
clot				cliff				
clap				clink				
clam				club				
clamp				cluck				
click				clump				
cleft				clag				
clan				clus				
clang				clob				

The big clock went tick, tock.

He will cling to the top of the cliff.

Initial Blend pl- as in planet

List 103					List 104				
pl-					pl-				
plan					plus				
plans					plum				
planet					plums				
plank					plug				
plonk					plugs				
plop					plump				
plops					plat				
plot					plun				
plots					plad				
plod					pleg				

Glen had the black plum.

The plump hen sat in the sun.

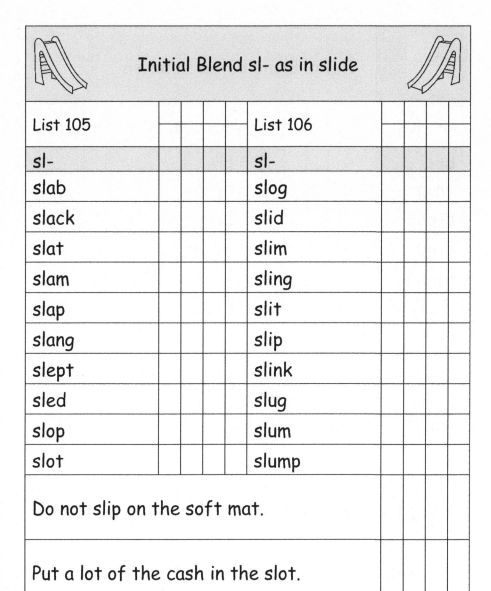

Initial Blend sl- as in slide

List 105					List 106				
sl-					sl-				
slab					slog				
slack					slid				
slat					slim				
slam					sling				
slap					slit				
slang					slip				
slept					slink				
sled					slug				
slop					slum				
slot					slump				

Do not slip on the soft mat.

Put a lot of the cash in the slot.

Initial Blend br- as in brush

List 107					List 108				
br-					br-				
brag					brim				
brags					brims				
bran					brunt				
brand					brisk				
brat					brink				
brig					brick				
bred					bricks				
bring					braf				
brings					brif				
bringing					brum				

Bring the brick to me.

The bun has lots of bran in it.

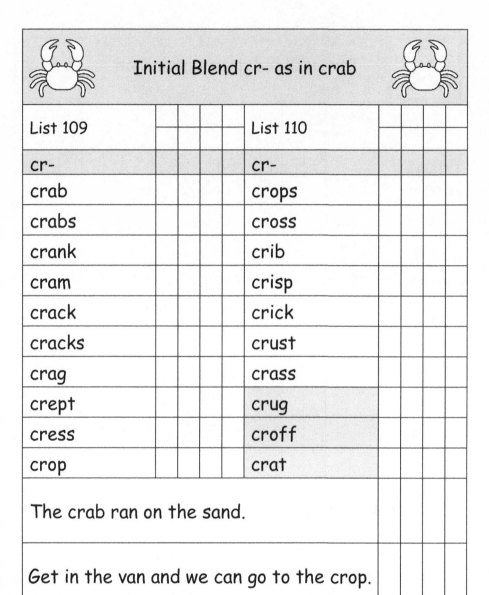

Initial Blend cr- as in crab							

List 109					List 110				
cr-					cr-				
crab					crops				
crabs					cross				
crank					crib				
cram					crisp				
crack					crick				
cracks					crust				
crag					crass				
crept					crug				
cress					croff				
crop					crat				

The crab ran on the sand.

Get in the van and we can go to the crop.

Initial Blend dr- as in dragon

List 111					List 112				
dr-					dr-				
drag					drinks				
drank					drug				
drab					drugs				
dram					drum				
dress					drums				
drop					drunk				
drill					drog				
drip					drif				
drift					drus				
drink					driv				

The tap went drip, drip, drip.

Do not bang the big black drum.

Initial Blend fr- as in frog

List 113				List 114			
fr-				fr-			
frog				frat			
frogs				frump			
from				frit			
frock				frig			
frond				frum			
frank				fren			
fret				frob			
frisk				freck			
frill				frab			
frills				friv			

The red fox ran from the hen shed.

The frog can hop and jump to the rock.

Initial Blend pr- as in present

List 115					List 116				
pr-					pr-				
print					prod				
prints					prods				
prat					press				
prats					prom				
prim					prick				
prig					pricks				
pram					prit				
prams					priv				
prank					prum				
pranks					prev				

Frank can get the frog to the pond.

The pin can prick me.

Initial Blend gr- as in grapes

List 117					List 118				
gr-					gr-				
gran					grub				
grand					grubs				
grab					gruff				
gram					grunt				
grid					grog				
grip					greg				
grin					grod				
grit					gruck				
grim					griff				
grill					gret				

The pink pig ran to the gran.

Grab the black grill in the hut.

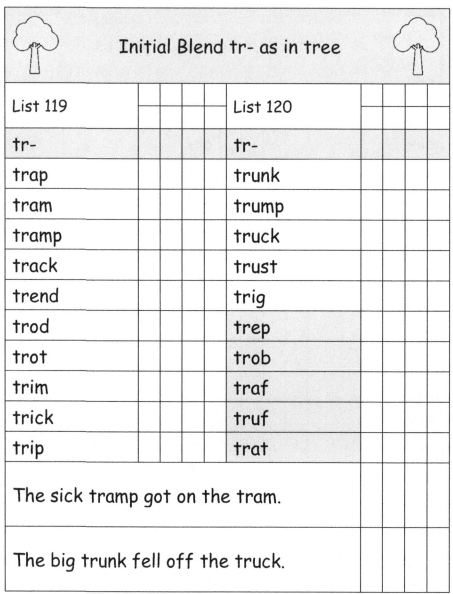

Initial Blend tr- as in tree

List 119					List 120				
tr-					tr-				
trap					trunk				
tram					trump				
tramp					truck				
track					trust				
trend					trig				
trod					trep				
trot					trob				
trim					traf				
trick					truf				
trip					trat				

The sick tramp got on the tram.

The big trunk fell off the truck.

Initial Blend wh- as in wheel

List 121				List 122			
wh-				wh-			
whip				Question words			
whips				what			
wheel				when			
wheels				where			
whizz				why			
whisk				which			
whiff				what			
whack				who			
Exception				whom			
whole				whose			

What did you do with the egg whisk?				

Whose whip is this?				

Initial Blend sw- as in swim

List 123						List 124					
sw-						sw-					
swim						swell					
swims						swop					
swill						swing					
swig						swings					
swift						swung					
swam						swit					
swank						swen					
swat						swog					
swan						swib					
swept						swuck					

The fish can swim in the pond.

The lad got on the swing and had fun.

Initial Blend tw- as in twins

List 125					List 126				
tw-					Mixed Word List				
twin					track				
twins					when				
twig					swell				
twigs					flat				
twist					glum				
twists					dwarf				
twill					clap				
twit					plug				
Exception					slam				
two					brat				
When will the tram go on the track?									
The twins ran on the track.									

Initial Blend sc- as in scarecrow

List 127					List 128				
sc-					Mixed Word List				
scab					drag				
scabs					fret				
scan					prod				
scant					grub				
scalp					trim				
scat					whip				
scam					swim				
scamp					twig				
scoff					brat				
scum					from				

The trim man ran from the cop.

Do not pick the scab on your skin.

Initial Blend sn- as in snow

List 129					List 130				
sn-					sn-				
snow					snip				
snows					snips				
snap					snob				
snaps					snug				
snack					snuff				
snacks					snil				
snag					snum				
snags					snef				
sniff					sniv				
sniffs					snut				

Get the snacks to the red tent.

The twig can snap in the wind.

Initial Blend sk- as in skull

List 131					List 132				
sk-					sk-				
skull					skins				
skulls					skip				
skunk					skips				
skunks					skit				
skulk					skill				
skid					skills				
skids					skaf				
skim					skib				
skimp					skut				
skin					sket				

A frog has a thin skin.

The skull is in the red skip.

Initial Blend sp- as in spot

List 133					List 134				
sp-					sp-				
spot					spells				
spots					spend				
span					spends				
spans					spud				
spank					spunk				
spanks					spag				
spat					spef				
sped					spob				
spent					spif				
spell					spum				

He has red spots on his neck.

Pam spent a lot of cash at the shop.

Initial Blend st- as in stop

List 135					List 136				
st-					st-				
stop					stilt				
stock					sting				
stamp					stick				
stank					stink				
stab					stiff				
stack					stub				
stag					stunt				
stem					stunts				
step					stuff				
still					stuck				

That big lamp cost a lot.

She must sit still on the step.

Initial Blend sm- as in smile

List 137					List 138				
sm-					sm-				
smile					smut				
smiles					smug				
smack					smat				
smacks					smaf				
small					smef				
smell					smip				
smells					smot				
smelt					smev				
smog					smod				
smock					smap				

The small dog can smell the cat.

I can smell the pink pig.

Unit 10: High-Frequency Words 41-60

List 139					List 140				
not					do				
then					me				
were					down				
go					dad				
little					big				
as					when				
no					it's				
mum					see				
one					looked				
them					very				

Mum looked at one of the little gifts.

When were we with them?

Unit 11: Final Consonant Blends Picture Chart

-nd	-nt	-nk
hand	ant	wink
-st	-sk	-mp
nest	desk	lamp
-lt	-ft	-ct
belt	gift	fact

Suggestions

- Say the word for the picture when looking at the picture.
- Read the word for the picture.
- Say the sound.
- Write the sounds.

Final Blend -nd as in hand

List 141					List 142				
-nd					-nd				
and					pond				
hand					ponds				
land					bond				
sand					wind				
end					winds				
lend					fund				
mend					funds				
fend					rand				
tend					hend				
bend					mand				

We can sit on the sand in the sun.

Do not bend the map as it can rip.

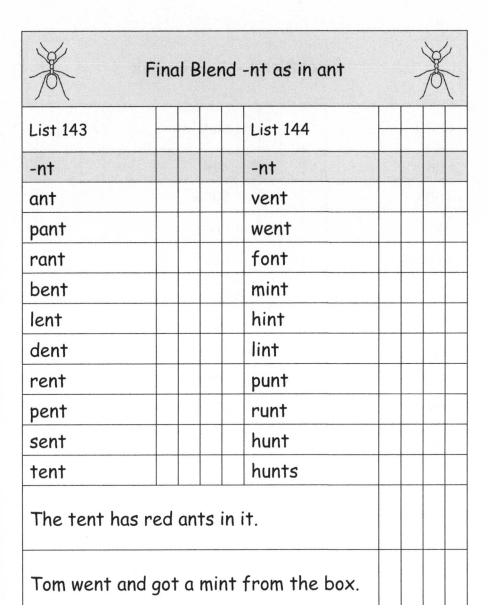

Final Blend -nt as in ant									
List 143					List 144				
-nt					-nt				
ant					vent				
pant					went				
rant					font				
bent					mint				
lent					hint				
dent					lint				
rent					punt				
pent					runt				
sent					hunt				
tent					hunts				

The tent has red ants in it.

Tom went and got a mint from the box.

Final Blend -nk as in wink

List 145					List 146				
-nk					-nk				
tank					sunk				
lank					link				
dank					mink				
rank					ink				
sank					rink				
bank					sink				
yank					wink				
bunk					blink				
hunk					stink				
junk					pink				

Sam got the pink pig in the shed.

Get on the bunk bed and have a nap.

Final Blend -st as in nest

List 147					List 148				
-st					-st				
nest					zest				
lest					lost				
best					cost				
jest					mist				
rest					fist				
fest					dust				
test					must				
vest					gust				
pest					rust				
west					just				

I lost my best pen in the tent.

It cost him a lot to get the best van.

Final Blend -sk as in desk

List 149					List 150				
-sk					-sk				
desk					task				
desks					tasks				
husk					bask				
tusk					cask				
dusk					risk				
musk					risks				
ask					lesk				
asks					wisk				
mask					tesk				
masks					lisk				

Pam will get me the mask.

The desk went in the big box.

Final Blend -mp as in lamp

List 151					List 152				
-mp					-mp				
lamp					sump				
ramp					dump				
tamp					rump				
camp					bump				
damp					hump				
hemp					jump				
romp					lump				
pomp					pump				
limp					femp				
imp					simp				

I have a lamp by my bed.

The sand by the pump is wet.

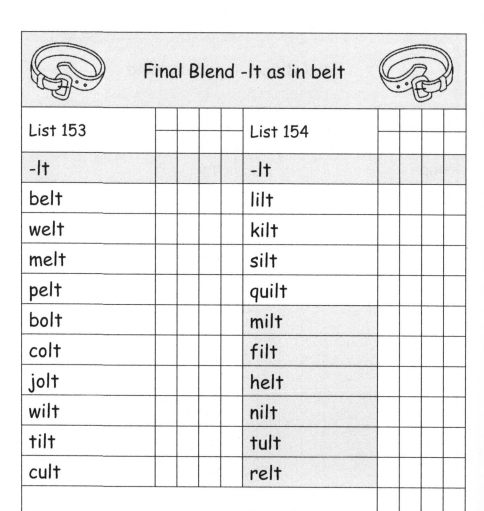

Final Blend -lt as in belt

List 153					List 154				
-lt					-lt				
belt					lilt				
welt					kilt				
melt					silt				
pelt					quilt				
bolt					milt				
colt					filt				
jolt					helt				
wilt					nilt				
tilt					tult				
cult					relt				

I must not gulp the hot milk.

The man has a long belt on.

Final Blend -ft as in gift

List 155					List 156				
-ft					-ft				
left					feft				
deft					neft				
soft					hoft				
loft					toft				
gift					nuft				
lift					luft				
rift					suft				
sift					fift				
tuft					hift				
raft					nift				

Lift the dog into the van.

I got a soft doll from Mum.

1+1=2 ✓	Final Blend -ct as in fact					1+1=2 ✓				
List 157					List 158					
-ct					Mixed Word List					
act					sand					
fact					hunt					
pact					link					
tact					rest					
sect					tusk					
duct					camp					
lect					fact					
rect					welt					
vect					lift					
luct					cost					
In my next act I will be a cat.										
The bunk bed did not cost a lot.										

Unit 12: High-Frequency Words 61-80

List 159					List 160				
look					get				
don't					just				
come					now				
will					came				
into					oh				
back					about				
from					got				
children					their				
him					people				
Mr					your				

Come and look at the people out there.

Oh, there it is!

-ss

kiss

-ff

cuff

-ll

doll

Suggestions

- Say the word for the picture when looking at the picture.
- Read the word for the picture.
- Say the sound.
- Write the sounds.

Double Consonant -ss as in kiss

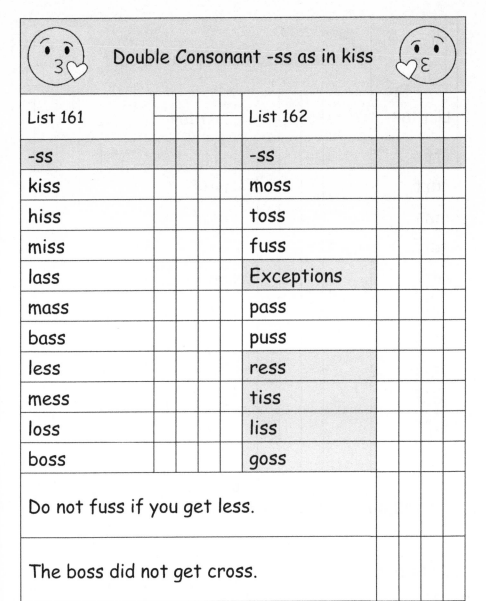

List 161					List 162				
-ss					-ss				
kiss					moss				
hiss					toss				
miss					fuss				
lass					Exceptions				
mass					pass				
bass					puss				
less					ress				
mess					tiss				
loss					liss				
boss					goss				

Do not fuss if you get less.

The boss did not get cross.

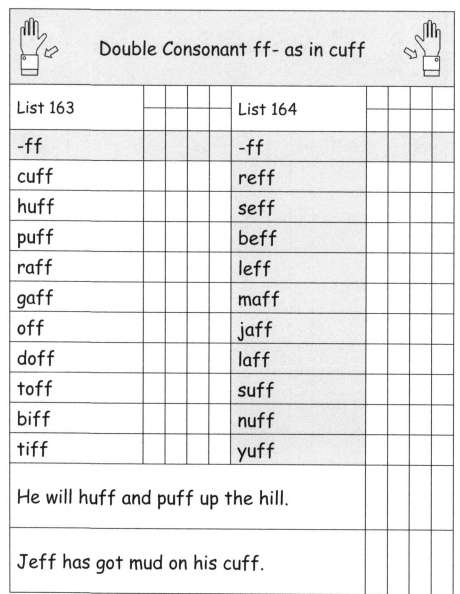

Double Consonant ff- as in cuff

List 163					List 164				
-ff					-ff				
cuff					reff				
huff					seff				
puff					beff				
raff					leff				
gaff					maff				
off					jaff				
doff					laff				
toff					suff				
biff					nuff				
tiff					yuff				

He will huff and puff up the hill.

Jeff has got mud on his cuff.

Double Consonant -ll as in bell

List 165					List 166				
-ll					-ll				
bell					will				
fell					all				
well					hall				
tell					ball				
sell					call				
doll					fall				
gull					Exceptions				
dull					pull				
hill					full				
pill					bull				

The -a- followed by -ll sounds like -orl.
The sound of -u- in pull sounds like -oo- in book.

Will ran to the hall to get his ball.

Double Consonants

List 167					List 168				
Mixed List					Mixed List				
doll					moss				
mass					guff				
huff					miss				
gull					all				
bass					kiss				
puff					well				
till					off				
cuff					will				
lass					hiss				
tell					hill				

That duck got stuck in the net.

The big gull sat on the deck.

Unit 14: High-Frequency Words 81-100

List 169					List 170				
put					if				
could					help				
house					Mrs				
old					called				
too					here				
by					off				
day					asked				
made					saw				
time					make				
I'm					an				
Mrs Bond went for a run up the hill.									
I have a red ball at my house.									

You have completed
Progress In Learning Book 1!

Good job!

Activities to Develop Learning

List 137 (sm-) has been used in some of the activities described below:

Reading

- Highlight the common sound evident in the list, using a highlighter, saying the sound as you find it.
- Read the lists and the sentences till accuracy and fluency is achieved.
- Type the word family into the search section of a computer-based programme such as 'Wordshark' to see approximately 40 games and activities to reinforce reading skills.
- Read the lists from left to right for more of a challenge.
- The tutor points to any word and the student reads it.

Reading Comprehension

- The tutor asks the student questions about what has been read in the sentences. (e.g. *What size was the dog? What did the small dog see? Do you prefer small or large dogs? Explain your answer. How do you think the cat feels when the dog is looking at it? Compare and contrast having a cat versus a dog as a pet. What do you think will happen next?*)
- The student makes up questions to ask the tutor about what has been read.

Written Language and Spelling

- The tutor asks the student questions based on the sentences and then the student writes the answers down.
- The reading lists may be used as spelling lists. Dictate the words to the student.
- The student can copy the list words.
- Students can build their own nonsense or true words with the same pattern.
- Use the sentences for dictation, in which the student rehearses, recalls and writes the sentence from memory.
- Encourage proofreading with the student checking the sentence. Say each word, pointing to it. Check that a capital letter and full stop has been used, that no words are missing and encourage self-correction of errors.
- Cut out the sentence from the book, cut the sentence into separate words, jumble, rebuild, then read or write the sentence.
- Read and copy out the sentences in a lined book. Do three a day.
- Students can make up their own sentences with the words.
- Expand the sentences - 'The small dog saw the small cat' → 'The small dog saw the small cat walking on the wall and started barking loudly at it'.
- Identify parts of speech such as nouns, verbs, adjectives, adverbs and conjunctions within the sentences.
- Type the word family into the search section of a computer-based programme such as 'Wordshark' to see games and activities to reinforce spelling skills.

Auditory Processing

- Create rhyming words. (*e.g. What words rhyme with 'small'?*)
- Identify the word which does not rhyme. (*e.g. Which word does not rhyme from these list words? 'small, ball, <u>storm</u>, call'*)
- Auditory memory for sentences. Repeat the sentence after the tutor. If necessary, write the sentence on a whiteboard for the student and rehearse it, then say the sentence again, rubbing out a word at a time until the student is able to recall the sentence with no visual clues.
- Missing word in sentences. (*e.g. What word is missing? The small _____ saw the small cat.*)
- Blend sounds together. (*e.g. 's-m-u-g'=?*)
- Analyse the sounds in the word. (*e.g. What four sounds can you hear in the word 'smug'?*)
- Manipulation of the sounds. (*e.g. Say 'smug'. Say it again but instead of 'sm' say 'gl'*)
- Identify the front, medial or end sound in a word. (*e.g. What sound do you hear in front of 'small'? What sound do you hear at the end of 'small'?*)

Progress In Learning (PIL) Phonic Skills Check

Instructions

The phonic skills check is administered to analyse a student's phonic knowledge prior to starting the workbook. In this way, placement within the programme may be determined and it provides valuable information as to where and why the student is struggling. Progress in reading and phonic knowledge can easily be measured by retesting the student's phonic skills.

1. Print out a copy of the STUDENT reading sheets and the TESTER scoring sheets. An A4 printout may be obtained from the website www.progressinlearning.co.nz

2. Laminating the STUDENT reading sheets is helpful so they can be reused.

3. Familiarise yourself with the test procedure before administering it to the student.

4. Record the name of the student and the date at the top of the TESTER recording sheets.

5. You have a choice of starting the test at the beginning, with sounds and words from Progress In Learning Book 1 or using the sheets for book 2 or 3. I personally like to start from book 1 as initial phonic knowledge may not have been firmly established and this may be an important contributing factor in the student not being able to read successfully.

6. Administer the phonic skills check again once the relevant reading workbook has been completed, using a different coloured pen, and compare results to measure progress. Progress to the next reading workbook.

Instructions for Progress In Learning Book 1

Single sounds

Ask the student to read the sounds of the alphabet from left to right, using letter sounds, not letter names. This is because the students need to be able to use letter sounds to sound out unknown words, as one decoding strategy. The student reads the lower-case letters, then the upper-case letters. Record any errors on your TESTER page, in the space above each letter.

Consonant-vowel-consonant (CVC) words and words with final and initial blends

Students read the words from left to right. Observe if the student is reading fluently and accurately. The underlined sound in each word indicates which sound was assessed. Record any errors on your TESTER page, in the space above each letter. Discontinue the skills check when approximately ten consecutive errors have been made. Score and record the number of sounds and list words read correctly in each section. If the student is unfamiliar with the sounds and is unable to read the words accurately and fluently, then they would benefit from using Progress In Learning Book 1. Supplementary resources such as games, worksheets, computer software and tactile products such as playdough and wooden alphabet letters are useful for teaching and reinforcing the sound/symbol relationships.

The First 100 High Frequency Words

The students read the words from left to right. Record responses or just mark responses correct or incorrect. Record the score at the top of the page. You now know exactly which high frequency words are known and which are not. These words are included in the Progress In Learning Book 1 and are essential for reading and writing.

Instructions for Progress In Learning Book 2

Word family lists

Students read the words from left to right. Observe if the student is reading fluently and accurately. The underlined sound in each word indicates which sound was assessed. Record any errors on your TESTER page, in the space above each word. Discontinue the skills check when approximately ten consecutive errors have been made. Record the score at the top of the page. You now know exactly which word families are known and which present a challenge to the student. These words are included in the Progress In Learning Book 2.

The Next 200 Common Words

The high frequency words table has been provided courtesy of Letters and Sounds, published by the UK Department for Education and Skills (DfES), Appendix 1 (pp.193-195), 2007.

The students read the words from left to right. Record responses in the space above each word. Record the score at the top of the page. You now know exactly which common words are known and which are not. These words are included in the Progress In Learning Book 2.

Instructions for Progress In Learning Book 3

Word family lists

Students read the words from left to right. Observe if the student is reading fluently and accurately. The underlined sound in each word indicates which sound was assessed. Record any errors on your TESTER page, in the space above each word. Discontinue the skills check when approximately ten consecutive errors have been made. Record the score at the top of the page. You now know exactly which common words are known and which are not. These words are included in the Progress In Learning Book 3.

Progress In Learning (PIL) Phonic Skills Check

TESTER Scoring Sheet for PIL Book 1 Sounds and Words

Name:_____ Date:_____ Score: /70

s	a	t	p	i	n	m
d	g	o	c	k	e	u
r	h	b	f	l	z	j
q	v	x	w	y		
S	A	T	P	I	N	M
D	G	O	C	K	E	U
R	H	B	F	L	Z	J
Q	V	X	W	Y		

---

h<u>a</u>m	l<u>o</u>t	p<u>e</u>g	h<u>u</u>t	f<u>i</u>n	l<u>og</u>
r<u>a</u>t	t<u>i</u>p	v<u>e</u>t	r<u>u</u>n	sa<u>nd</u>	le<u>nt</u>
bli<u>nk</u>	ri<u>sk</u>	<u>fl</u>at	<u>gr</u>ab	<u>sm</u>ug	<u>sn</u>ag

If the student is unable to read or write the above sounds and words fluently and accurately, they need Progress In Learning Book 1.

TESTER Scoring Sheet for PIL Book 1 Words

Name:_____ Date:_____ Score: /100

First 100 High-frequency Words

(These are included in PIL Book 1)

the	and	a	to	said
in	he	I	of	it
was	you	they	on	she
is	for	at	his	but
that	with	all	we	can
are	up	had	my	her
what	there	out	this	have
went	be	like	some	so
not	then	were	go	little
as	no	mum	one	them
do	me	down	dad	big
when	it's	see	looked	very
look	don't	come	will	into
back	from	children	him	Mr
get	just	now	came	oh
about	got	their	people	your
put	could	house	old	too
by	day	made	time	I'm
if	help	Mrs	called	here
off	asked	saw	make	an

Progress In Learning (PIL) Phonic Skills Check

TESTER Scoring Sheet for PIL Book 2 Words

Name:_____ Date:_____ Score: /48

shed	rush	them	cloth	chest	stack
dolphin	hang	swing	gong	lung	quill
whip	what	flask	last	rate	blame
eve	theme	hike	glide	slope	flute
flee	stay	tie	snail	loaf	steam
clue	grow	spoil	round	crew	bread
shook	crawl	joy	crown	tooth	haunt
nerve	stir	turn	farm	short	fly

If the student is unable to read or write the above sounds and words fluently and accurately, they need Progress In Learning Book 2.

TESTER Scoring Sheet for PIL Book 2 Words

Name:_____ Date:_____ Score: /200

Next 200 Common Words

(These are included in PIL Book 2)

water	away	good	want	over	how
did	man	going	where	would	or
took	school	think	home	who	didn't
ran	know	bear	can't	again	cat
long	things	new	after	wanted	eat
everyone	our	two	has	yes	play
take	thought	dog	well	find	more
I'll	round	tree	magic	shouted	us
other	food	fox	through	way	been
stop	must	red	door	right	sea
these	began	boy	animals	never	next
first	work	lots	need	that's	baby
fish	gave	mouse	something	bed	may
still	found	live	say	soon	night
narrator	small	car	couldn't	three	head
king	town	I've	around	every	garden
fast	only	many	laughed	let's	much
suddenly	told	another	great	why	cried
keep	room	last	jumped	because	even
am	before	gran	clothes	tell	key
fun	place	mother	sat	boat	window
sleep	feet	morning	queen	each	book
its	green	different	let	girl	which
inside	run	any	under	hat	snow
air	trees	bad	tea	top	eyes
fell	friends	box	dark	grandad	there's
looking	end	than	best	better	hot
sun	across	gone	hard	floppy	really
wind	wish	eggs	once	please	thing
stopped	ever	miss	most	cold	park
lived	birds	duck	horse	rabbit	white
coming	he's	river	liked	giant	looks
use	along	plants	dragon	pulled	we're
fly	grow				

Progress In Learning (PIL) Phonic Skills Check

TESTER Scoring Sheet for PIL Book 3 Words

Name:_____ Date:_____ Score: /65

story   fetch   pinch   thrill   scrap   strand

sprain   splash   squeak   shrimp   blind   cold

cereal   citizen   cylinder   concert   voice   price

place   they'll   you've   where's   imagine   strange

wedge   manage   comb   column   knit   palm

yolk   whistle   wrinkle   taste   might   expect

marker   sunflower   newspaper   untidy   beware

remain   cheerful   costly   truthfully   richness

lotion   expansion   conclusion   financial   sponge

pilot   although   flair   glare   squire   cure

shore   wander   traffic   swarm   umbrella

worship   raisin   needle

If a student is unable to read or write the above sounds
and words fluently and accurately, they need Progress In
Learning Book 3.

Teaching Notes

STUDENT Reading Sheet for PIL Book 1 Sounds and Words

s	a	t	p	i	n	m
d	g	o	c	k	e	u
r	h	b	f	l	z	j
q	v	x	w	y		
S	A	T	P	I	N	M
D	G	O	C	K	E	U
R	H	B	F	L	Z	J
Q	V	X	W	Y		

---

ham	lot	peg	hut	fin	log
rat	tip	vet	run	sand	lent
blink	risk	flat	grab	smug	snag

> If I am unable to read or write the above sounds and words fluently and accurately, I need Progress In Learning Book 1.

STUDENT Reading Sheet for PIL Book 1 Words

First 100 High-frequency Words
(These are included in PIL Book 1)

the	and	a	to	said
in	he	I	of	it
was	you	they	on	she
is	for	at	his	but
that	with	all	we	can
are	up	had	my	her
what	there	out	this	have
went	be	like	some	so
not	then	were	go	little
as	no	mum	one	them
do	me	down	dad	big
when	it's	see	looked	very
look	don't	come	will	into
back	from	children	him	Mr
get	just	now	came	oh
about	got	their	people	your
put	could	house	old	too
by	day	made	time	I'm
if	help	Mrs	called	here
off	asked	saw	make	an

STUDENT Reading Sheet for PIL Book 2 Words

shed	rush	them	cloth	chest	stack
dolphin	hang	swing	gong	lung	quill
whip	what	flask	last	rate	blame
eve	theme	hike	glide	slope	flute
flee	stay	tie	snail	loaf	steam
clue	grow	spoil	round	crew	bread
shook	crawl	joy	crown	tooth	haunt
nerve	stir	turn	farm	short	fly

If I am unable to read or write the above sounds and words fluently and accurately, I need Progress In Learning Book 2.

Next 200 Common Words
(These are included in PIL Book 2)

water	away	good	want	over	how
did	man	going	where	would	or
took	school	think	home	who	didn't
ran	know	bear	can't	again	cat
long	things	new	after	wanted	eat
everyone	our	two	has	yes	play
take	thought	dog	well	find	more
I'll	round	tree	magic	shouted	us
other	food	fox	through	way	been
stop	must	red	door	right	sea
these	began	boy	animals	never	next
first	work	lots	need	that's	baby
fish	gave	mouse	something	bed	may
still	found	live	say	soon	night
narrator	small	car	couldn't	three	head
king	town	I've	around	every	garden
fast	only	many	laughed	let's	much
suddenly	told	another	great	why	cried
keep	room	last	jumped	because	even
am	before	gran	clothes	tell	key
fun	place	mother	sat	boat	window
sleep	feet	morning	queen	each	book
its	green	different	let	girl	which
inside	run	any	under	hat	snow
air	trees	bad	tea	top	eyes
fell	friends	box	dark	grandad	there's
looking	end	than	best	better	hot
sun	across	gone	hard	floppy	really
wind	wish	eggs	once	please	thing
stopped	ever	miss	most	cold	park
lived	birds	duck	horse	rabbit	white
coming	he's	river	liked	giant	looks
use	along	plants	dragon	pulled	we're
fly	grow				

STUDENT Reading Sheet for PIL Book 3 Words

story   fetch   pinch   thrill   scrap   strand

sprain   splash   squeak   shrimp   blind   cold

cereal   citizen   cylinder concert   voice   price

place   they'll   you've   where's   imagine   strange

wedge   manage   comb   column   knit   palm

yolk   whistle   wrinkle   taste   might   expect

marker   sunflower newspaper untidy   beware

remain   cheerful costly   truthfully richness

lotion   expansion conclusion financial sponge

pilot   although flair   glare   squire   cure

shore   wander   traffic   swarm   umbrella

worship   raisin   needle

If I am unable to read or write the above sounds and words fluently and accurately, I need Progress In Learning Book 3.

Teaching Notes

Picture and Rime Charts

It is vital that there be automatic sound/symbol association with the alphabet, blend, and rime charts. Practice reading, writing, and saying the charts frequently. Start each lesson with reading a picture chart and rime chart related to the page of reading that the student is doing.

Phonics

Words and their families are presented in a structured and cumulative way. Pseudo words have been added as practicing the reading of nonsense words is a good way to build decoding skills and is useful in training phonemic awareness. Interference having to do with the meaning or spelling of a word is eliminated. There is also more of a focus on sounds than letter names.

High-Frequency Words

The high-frequency words are, according to international research, the words used most often when you read or write, so they are important. They are listed according to how often they are used. This means that the words in list 88 are used more often that the words in list 89. The words correlate exactly with the high-frequency word lists presented in SparkleBox, so the relevant flashcards, wall charts, displays etc. are readily available, for free.

The students need to learn to read and write them quickly and accurately. Encourage the students to learn in a multisensory way - hearing, seeing, saying and writing the word. Some children may need or want to build the words.

Materials and activities to construct words include:

- Playdough
- Plasticine
- Wiki Stix
- Magnetic letters
- Alphabet letters
- Write the words on scrap paper, in salt, powder jelly, on concrete with chalk, on a whiteboard, on a magnetic board, or using colourful pens
- Type or find the words within a computer software program such as 'Wordshark' and complete the associated activities for further reinforcement.

Lesson Format

Goal Setting for the Lesson

Revision of a Picture Sound Chart

Revision of a Sound Chunks Chart

Revision of High-Frequency Words

Read the Word Lists

Activities from the back of the book

Feedback and Record Progress on the Progress Chart

Acknowledgements

- The First 100 High-Frequency Words table and Next 200 Common Words table has been provided courtesy of Letters and Sounds, published by the UK Department for Education and Skills (DfES), Appendix 1 (pp.193-195), 2007.

- Excerpts and permission to use resources granted by www.sparklebox.co.uk. Resources are © Copyright.

- SparkleBox Teacher Resources Limited (UK).

- Kyle Esterhuizen, for designing the lovely cover.

- Laura-Rose Wiechern, for providing attractive interior images and the author photograph.

- Rosanna Hosseini, for her excellent formatting and proofreading of the manuscript.

Personal Comments

"The Progress In Learning series are an affordable set of resources, providing a structured, systematic method for assisting struggling learners to focus on sounds in words. I often recommend these resources to students to assist with developing their phonological awareness, which is an essential foundation for literacy skills."

Angela Neville

BED (Teaching, Med Psych - First Class Honours)

Registered Educational Psychologist

* * * * * * * *

"Highlands Intermediate School has used the Progress In Learning workbooks for several years, with great success. The programme certainly provided the students with good strategies for reading and the books were able to be used by the teacher aide and the parent. The students gained self-confidence and they made steady progress."

Kathryn Hooper

Acting Principal

Highlands Intermediate School

* * * * * * * *

"Kim Morris has spent many years working with those who struggle with literacy. She is committed to utilising a range of strategies to help children succeed with reading and writing. Her book presents a sequential and integrative approach for teaching the skills of decoding and word attack. The tasks are presented in a clear, logical way and are easy to complete in a short time frame.

My son and I worked together on these activities and after 6 months there was marked improvement in his decoding skills and confidence in reading. He now engages actively with the text and is beginning to enjoy reading.

When children struggle with literacy it is likely they will face many challenges during their years of education. We should give them the chance to discover how they learn best so they are empowered to maximise their learning potential.

This book is a valuable resource for parents, teachers and those who need extra literacy support."

Dr Catherine Rawlinson

Senior Lecturer in Education

* * * * * * * *

"As a SPELD Teacher I have found the Progress In Learning books to be an invaluable tool. Children learn to identify the patterns within words and this helps them to read similar words."

Kate Caldwell

SPELD Teacher

* * * * * * * *

Made in the USA
Monee, IL
08 October 2021